Partners In Purpose

Poems

and

Spoken Word
Video Book

Edopoetics
Publishing

ISBN: 978-0-57887375-6

Editor: Carla DuPont
Cover Design: Edo Walker III

Edopoetics Publishing LLC
11950 Erwin St
North Hollywood, CA 91606

Schools & Businesses

Edopoetics Publishing books are available
at quantity discounts with bulk.

For more information please email
sales@edowalker.com

Dedication

I dedicate this book to the memory of my mother.

My first and favorite teacher as well as the artist who introduced me

to the world of poetry. Because of you I am forever a student of life.

Thank you,

Amanda Jean Walker

Your voice carries on!

Spoken Word
Video Book

We truly live in unique and exciting times. Today's technology is constantly advancing and providing a level of convenience that previous generations never imagined. Like many people, I have a love/hate relationship with the written word. I love to read, but I only have the time or feel like doing the mental work reading demands sometimes. Reading poetry requires an elevated level of patience, especially with a unique book that contains many specially designed poems. Instead of buckling down to read, many of us would rather listen, especially during those times when we are trying to unwind. By utilizing today's literary technological trends, you have the option of reading, listening, or watching.

To enhance your experience, I have added a spoken word video book that allows you to have a video and audio performance of the poems.

You will find a QR code that contains videos of me performing the spoken word version of each verse. You can access your video book by scanning the code using your phone. I also included a recent and random folder to access my exclusive visual content.

Partners In Purpose

WWW.EdoWalker.Com

"Partners In Purpose," is a one of a kind collection of love and relationship poems. Each poem is uniquely structured to be its own story and lend to the overall theme that love is a journey and you will encounter pleasure, pain, and providence along the way. This book is a unique fusion of classic poetry and contemporary hip hop, that creates a distinctive reading experience that is both captivating and relatable. It's a perfect blend of the old and the new that's designed to speaks to your heart. It's a literal and visual work that captures the essence of the highs and lows that most of us have experienced in our love cycles. This book isn't just about artistry and entertainment. It's about scratching beyond the attraction surface. To this day, L.L. Cool J's "I Need Love is one of my favorite songs. If you've ever wanted to read the lyrics to some of your favorite love songs. Or have your partner read some captivating words to you. This book can help you accomplish just that and more.

This book is the perfect escape to enjoy some quality time. There are love enhancers and reinforcers woven into the pages that will transport you into a world of consideration and romantic appreciation. It covers first impressions and first dates to blocked calls and don't ever call me again. There are even some lust at first sight and nobody else has to know poems. It encompasses all the experiences that shape our expectations on the road to long term commitment. For many people marriage is the destination and for others it's viewed as a beginning. I believe this book can be a resource for everyone that desires a committed relationship. Afterall, it takes loving with intention to operate in a space of passion and purpose that creates LOVEGEVITY.

Most of all "Partners in Purpose," is here to remind you that you're not alone. Love is a journey that requires an abundance of effort and patience. If you're willing to do the work your best love life is ahead of you and this book is a road map to help you get there. We're all trying to reach the next level in life and in love. For those who are soul mate searching this is a must-read asset to successfully attract and keep a partner in purpose.

CONTENTS

Expression 1: One Track Love

Expression 2: As You Are

Expression 3: Fractions

Expression 4: Handcuff Heaven

Expression 5: Bliss

41. Anything
42. Bliss
43. When Love Is Real
44. Fortunate Hearts
45. Beyond Expectations
46. Vulnerable
47. Good Thing
48. Perfect Alignment
49. This Is Love
50. Partners In Purpose

Edopoetics IG

Will You Be My Partner In Purpose?

The idea of having a "partner in crime" has been romanticized in popular culture, finding a love that you will ride or die for. There is poetic beauty in that level of commitment but often those types of relationships are transactional and eventually become one sided. Resulting in short term pleasure and lacking a deeper sense of purpose. What most of us really want is help mate that is committed to our growth and evolution individually and as a couple. A person that wants to help you become the best version of yourself. Through the unique structure and rhythm of each poem, you'll discover the beauty and complexity of modern relationships. You'll gain a deeper understanding of the importance of emotional maturity, intentionality, and the power of love as a tool for personal growth and connection.

That's the philosophy behind Partners in Purpose, a collection of love and relationship poems that celebrates the beauty of intentional, growth-focused partnerships. Whether you're single, starting a new relationship, or looking to enhance an existing one, these pages offer valuable insights and inspiration for cultivating a healthy and fulfilling partnership.

Partners In Purpose will always believe that it's possible for "Team Us" to accomplish anything together.

To anyone that believes love is about helping each other get to the next level I invite you to dive into these poetic pages.

I hope you enjoy the journey.

Witnessed your heart descend like a shooting star

all because your last man was so subpar

he didn't know he could touch your soul

if he took the time to kiss your scars

I'm anywhere you need me

no matter how far

– Your *Partner In Purpose*

Expression 1: Featured Poem

I'm Sure

I'M SURE
THAT FLAMES FROM THE SUN
WILL BURN LONGER THAN RIVERS RUN
I'M SURE THAT YOUR SMILE
WILL BE THE ONLY THING I NEVER FORGET
SINCE YOU'RE THE MOST
AMAZING WOMAN I'VE EVER MET

I'M SURE A GOOD THING BUILDS
SO LET'S PLANT LOVE CROPS
IN OUR EMOTIONAL FIELDS

Expression 1

One
Track Love

Video

Poems

1. # <u>Blink</u>

Sometimes I stare too much

    even though my mother

        taught to me better

She also told me

    if you ever find an angel

        keep her in your eyes forever

So please excuse me

    and blink twice

        then I'll return

            from the paradise

                I've found in your eyes

Surreal

You light up my darkness
something about your presence
has brought my heart
out of hiding
and I tried fighting
but there's no denying
that our stars are aligning
A galaxy so inviting
that my body is igniting
I mean words just can't explain
the way you get next to me
wait let me try, this is
better than sex baby

We need each other
to make it through
prisoners of the heart
you're a part of me
I share a bond with you

Sometimes it feels like
we sip the same wine
and think the same thoughts
at the same time
it's so natural the way
our worlds combine
Our love is free will
you know it's real
when kisses heal
and every touch
gives you chills
the way this feels
is so surreal

3.

<u>One Track Love</u>

When two hearts
have a common objective
distant opinions don't seem
to mean as much
as your lover's calming touch
while kisses crash and crush
outside words come to a hush

You find yourself lost
in space and time
by something that feels so good
it should be a crime
creating a climate of addiction
and love is the only prescription
warning that side effects may apply
like never wanting to say goodbye
or needing to open windows
in the center of the winter
hanging imaginary signs
that say 'do not enter'

Hearts are complete
when a couple sleeps
with tangled feet and dream
to the rhythm of beating hearts
so close an artist
couldn't draw them apart
try but can't tell by the naked eye
need a magnifying lens
to see where one body ends
and the other begins
see love never pretends
it consumes then ascends

Revolutions

I can feel the depth of your love
from two planets away

Most beautiful soul in the entire Milky Way
answer to every word I pray

Your star orbits my heart like the earth
revolves around the Sun you are my chosen one

I need you next to me this is beyond ecstasy
since you unleash the best in me

I'm engulfed in the calm of your rage
trapped in the space of a distant gaze

More patience than Venus days
solar kisses beyond a lunar phase

They heal my broken ways
writing on the wall of destiny's page

5.

I'm Sure

I'm sure
that flames from the Sun
will burn longer than rivers run
I'm sure that your smile
will be the only thing I never forget
since you're the most
amazing woman I've ever met

I'm sure a *Good Thing* builds
so let's plant love crops
in our emotional fields
to ensure our hearts yield
a lifeline that never stops
you're my eternal rock
our commitment locks and seals

I'm sure that love is enough
you make me happy just because
our intimacy exposes every part of me
I can kiss you for an eternity
if fate doesn't have an expiration date
you can cover my heart and color my stars
with stripes that will never fade away
I love you 40 hours a day
from 88 states away

I'm sure that one day
when the oceans are gone
dusk and dawn become one
the Earth shall kiss the Sun
and our love will still drift along
I'm sure

Lunar

Nebula clouds and black holes
consuming everything in sight
but they can't dull my guiding light
just like a dream you loom
deceivingly sky falling in the night
close enough to pull you into my arms
but a million miles out of range
you are the ghost
I want to haunt my heart

My cosmic compass, you are a full moon
the light at the end of the tunnel
orbiting my star and tidal-locking my love
your gravitational pull balances my emotional ocean

Your beauty is like a total eclipse
I can't see anything but you
cycling through love phases
light that illuminates my soul
the outside world isn't so cold
when you have someone to hold
dancing to the music of a meteor shower
a concert of hearts is a teardrop symphony
I want to be part of your song
let me exist in your galaxy

My cosmic compass, you are a full moon
the light at the end of the tunnel
orbiting my star and tidal-locking my love
your gravitational pull balances my emotional ocean

<u>Relief</u>

If you're TIRED of
doing this on your own

help has ARRIVED
I'm here to make
my PRESENCE known

A GOOD WOMAN
should never be alone
let me turn your heart
into my love zone

you've done enough
now it's my turn
to take care of home

I watched your
love interest accrue
close those old accounts
and start over new

now sit back and relax
RELIEF was long overdue

he didn't see your VALUE
but the cost of SANITY isn't worth
trying making sense of a fool

you can fall into my arms
and just lose yourself

I was MADE to love you
so with every second
you INCREASE my WEALTH

Temptation

Your voice calms my heart
like virgin eyes
introduced to timeless art
it's a song of strength
that carries me
when times are hard

When the enticing words
in my head attempt
a physical escape
the power of love protects me
from the entrapment
of desire's rape
you're my third eye
detecting temptation
in every form and shape

In the absence of your presence
the body of temptation
transforms into sound
bending my ears
with whispers abound

But every time I fall
a balloon of love
consumes me before
I touch the ground

your strength is so dynamic
it won't even allow me
to let my own self
down

your strength is so dynamic
it won't even allow me
to let my own self
down

your strength is so dynamic
it won't even allow me
to let my own self
down

9. <u>Swipe Life</u>

Soulmate searching the digital sea
plenty of fish out there but can you land
the whale of your dating destiny
each swipe is a roll of the dice
she's swiping for a husband
hoping he's swiping for a wife
they're swiping for a better life
you're trying to swipe precise
searching for eyes that entice
a bio that's honest and concise
damn that smile is nice
oops you might have swiped them twice

Swipe momentum pushed you past a perfect 10
one wrong swipe and your forever love can end
before it has a chance to begin
this swipe life means having to sort through
the pretend and search for the truth hidden within
digital deception is perception
you become an expert of photo inspection
question every camera angle selection
so much manipulation and content correction
we all delete apps and then double back
hoping to make a genuine connection

If you're asked about how you met
you'd probably say in traffic
since it was in a space of digital gridlock
both of you south paw swiping away
an army of photos hoping the right ones
will lead to the right one and the gaze
of first contact can make opposites attract
and two hearts have the confidence
to gain momentum and never look back

All Gas & No Brakes

My crooked smile
will forever KISS you straight

true love is a religion
so I pass poems
like a collection plate

always shoot my shot
more misses than makes

all GAS and no BRAKES
LOVE COLLISIONS LEFT IN MY WAKE

heartaches and heartbreaks
but I still have faith
I'll find my SOULMATE

I am who I am
trying to escape the hate
I never stop for red lights

BECAUSE LOVE CAN'T WAIT

100 miles per hour
all GAS and no BRAKES
doing WHATEVER it takes
to control my own FATE

fast times and hot dates
chasing a shooting star
racing across states

ALL GAS AND NO BRAKES

Expression 2

Featured Poem

Don't Lead Me On

Love her or leave her
in peace
with sugar on top
and a pretty please
don't lead her on
just let her be - keep it moving
there's nothing there for you to see
you have more to lose than you do to gain
don't lead her on and she'll do the same
there is no need for shame
just go in your phone
and delete her name

Expression 2

As You Are

Video

Poems

11. <u>Cheapskate</u>

When we sleep
we're both alone
laying there together
despite the love is gone
I say it's cheaper
to keep her
but the truth is my heart
won't let me leave her

Trapped in a love
we do not have
it doesn't make sense
no matter how you do the math
and I know she's missing yesterday
still can't figure out why she stays
but we keep holding on
hoping the radio plays our song

We both know it's wrong
it's so wrong
and still we stay
to promote love lies
another day
just can't see things
being any other way
and I pray our heart
wounds heal with time
the price of regret is never kind
and refunds aren't an option
in love's broken design

Echoes of Tomorrow

Promise me
promise
that you
will always love me
and the answer to your heart's sorrow
is holding me   like there's   no tomorrow
give me your   whispers   and all your fears
I'll keep them safe…………..no other eyes……………no other ears

keep staring   too long   offering me the world
and stealing kisses   until the   night is gone
be my light when the sky is gray
love me completely   tomorrow and today
hold me when you can't find   the words to say
stay close and I'll know   you love me anyway
save my kisses in the center of your soul
use them to keep the spark
so our fire never goes cold

Stay with me
and together we'll grow
tomorrow's sun………maybe yes………or it may be no
but if I'll have your love…………………………is all I want to know
be my eyes when I can't see close in the light or the dark with me
appreciate my feel and remember my touch
I can never have enough
so try and love me too much
a promise of the heart is all I ask
cherish the face without the mask
see love isn't complex
it's simple and plain
as long as our love
always remains the same
so love me tomorrow as you do today

13. <u>As You Are</u>

It's possible the world is a perfect circle
and melancholy is best defined by the color purple
money may be the answer to material stress
but if you spend your life trapping hearts
then more is less when it comes to love
let's remove the question marks and never guess
you may never be a millionaire or movie star
still, I accept you just as you are

So you made a mistake, multiply mine by ten
these things happen every now and then
feelings get hurt but love understands
just leave the past in the past
that's where it belongs
trust in each other
instead of yesterday's wrongs
sometimes you've got to jump first
and ask questions later
or live erratic to make lifelines straighter
you can get close to a distant heart
by traveling somewhere far
and still I love you just as you are

Too often we have to learn the hard way
that love isn't always shared by lovers
and it's better to share your life
before sharing your covers
one thing that life teaches you
is no matter how well someone speaks to you
trust is held in the way they treat you
when love is pure the road is rougher
then you appreciate the past
the more you have suffered
so history never repeats you raise the bar
regardless I love you today and always
for being exactly as you are

Rescue Me

Each kiss cures
indulge and calm
your nerves
it's a natural attraction
that compels my verbs
it feels like you speak
with metallic words
and my eyes are like magnets
the way they attach to your curves
you're not happy, well I can give you
everything your heart deserves

No need to worry
relax and   enjoy the ride
I'll provide the   fire that warms
all the cold   spaces inside
it's impossible for   you to conceal
the truth indefinitely   because the eyes
reveal a secret; they say
RESCUE ME

Your heart is hurting
and I'm the answer it seeks
just take my hand
and allow love to flow free
if pain is your prison I'll be the key
see I could never
promise a woman love
that I couldn't give her
and I'd never offer
my heart if I couldn't deliver
you've been hurt before
even a blind man could see
it's written all over your face
it says…. RESCUE ME

15. <u>Mystique</u>

My mind has grown **weak**

can't convince myself I don't love you

it's a losing battle since my heart must **speak**

a complex conflict can't explain

the questions surrounding love's **mystique**

even when I try it's impossible to **stray**

because my heart cries out

I can't even last a **day**

a desire for love

always brings me back **again**

when my ego screams let go

my heart doesn't stop to **listen**

the damage has been done

it's your love I'm **missing**

now I know that crimes against

the heart can only be solved by

returning to love's gentle **kissing**

Don't Lead Me On

LOVE HER
or leave her
in peace
WITH SUGAR ON TOP
and a pretty please
don't lead her on
just let her be - keep it moving
there's nothing there for you to see
you have more to lose than you do to gain
don't lead her on and she'll do the same

there is no need for shame
just go in your phone
and delete her name
TRUTH BE TOLD
she's not in your lane
you're not even playing
the same damn game
YOUR SOUR KISSES
can't exist in her candy rain
she works too hard
to be contained
by someone mundane

Stop blocking the view
allow her to be seen
so a king can pursue
IT'S CHESS NOT CHECKERS
a woman of value may not be
the right fit for you
queens can make your
dreams come true
but if you don't
TREAT THEM RIGHT
your ass is
THROUGH

Entanglements

Blinded by
an **intoxicating** LUST
I'm so **addicted** to
your WHISPERS hushed
but you belong to someone else
and I shouldn't be **craving** you this much
always on my mind but out of sight
my guilty appetite a temptation I can't fight
even Superman has his KRYPTONITE
but our two **wrongs** only make him right
cause what's done in the DARK
always comes to **light**

Forbidden desires have no edges and no end
deleted texts and **hidden** folders
sexy photos stashed within
sinning every time I hit send
my heart has to **escape** these entanglements

Betrayed by the mirror
 I'm staring into
  the EYES of a **stranger**
   why am I making
    the same **mistakes** with you
     putting us both in **danger**
      your man is emotionally INADEQUATE
       but I **over stand** his anger
        sins of the skin
         an ego battle **between** men
          eventually our **reckless** actions
           Will end on a red table
            WEB of **entanglements**

Quarantine

A lonely heart
is driving me insane
when the depression came
I tried to drink away the pain
I closed my eyes and tried
to dream through the mundane
isolation is getting the best of me
this pandemic is taking the rest of me
baby I wish you were next to me
I'd even kiss you if we were masked up
wouldn't allow an opportunity to pass up

While the whole world is locked away
will you be my Quarantine Bae
so we can stay inside and play
make these blues fade to grey
I'll satisfy you all night and day

Suffering in the silence
of social compliance
I'm slipping into defiance
sipping on liquid gold like King Midas
waiting on science to defeat this virus
are we contagious, the tests say no
one thing is for sure I need you close
you're my vaccine and I need a dose
hope the spread of this pandemic slows

While the whole world is locked away
will you be my Quarantine Bae
so we can stay inside and play
make these blues fade to grey
I'll satisfy you all night and day

<u>Heart Hustler</u>

Looks like
temptation was stronger
than us   and pleasure
meant more than   securing our trust
just greedy eyes chasing lust and materiel stuff
I spied you were trying to keep me in cuffs
with a mouthful of lies, another bluff
the truth was never enough
it was fake love if you
needed a secret lover
a double agent I blew your cover
goodbye spy   no longer will I try
you can run game   on the others
but my mother didn't   raise no suckers
when karma catches   up to you
I hope your   ass suffers

At 1st I was blind   to your moves
shook up believing   love had rules
space in my heart   your lies took up
I bought into a lie   guess I paid love's due
two wrongs won't   make it right
so now my soul   plays the blues
right or wrong   there's no limits to love
anyway I'm too   confused to choose
I found gold   you know the kind
that fades   on fools

but it's cool   because you'll
never find another   who can love you
like I have   loved you
smothered   desire's fire
with the   covers   you shared
with that other mutherfucka

Theory of Relativity

As long as the **clouds** dance above
birds and bees will keep making **love**
you'll be the only **one** I'm thinking of

Since a thought can never be **undone**
the science of the **heavens** and earth are one
every heart is a star that can **rage** like a Sun

A COSMIC INTROSPECTIVE IS SUBJECTIVE

I **believe** love is
a metaphysical connection
beyond **Attraction** and **Affection**

We're part of God's plan
light **manifesting** emotion
between a woman and man

Circle of love 360 degrees
we share a sacred bond **invariably**
in the **theory of relativity**
you are my gravity

Not even **Einstein** could divide
the **space** between you and me

Expression 3: Featured Poem

Crossroads

INTUITION TOLD ME

THAT SOMETHING WASN'T RIGHT

EVEN THOUGH MY HEART

PUT UP A FIGHT

WHAT'S DONE IN THE DARK

ALWAYS COMES TO LIGHT

Expression 3

Fractions

Video

Poems

Missed Calls

Still don't know why
I tried to convince myself to live a lie

So used to being deceived
wasn't ready to close my eyes
and let my soul believe

Hypnotized by lust
I wasn't ready to trust

Or to adjust my moral compass
allow me to become us
wasn't ready to forfeit lust
and pursue love's rush

To face temptation and rise above
I wasn't ready for love

At the right time
I was the wrong man
lost in the devil's plan

Instead of listening to my heart
I tried holding water with my hands
now I'm drowning in quicksand

Oblivious to the fruit of the tree
loving with my eyes and indulging
in everything that appealed to me

Dancing in darkness, blind men
aren't the only ones unable to see
the king within hadn't grown to be

Wasn't ready for love
when love was calling me

Scales

LOVE

in, love out
you keep
confusing me

COME

in, get out
are you leaving
or choosing me

STANDING ON

a scale of emotion
and I'm losing
my balance

SAYING GOODBYE

is my ultimate challenge

THIS LOVE THING

is worse than insanity
but nothing sounds
crazier than me

BEING WITHOUT

MY BABY

Acting Class

The Setting – a play
The Plot – heart attacking
The Theme – have it your way
The Title – art of heart trapping

Every relationship
has problems and mistakes
are bound to happen
but this drama wasn't by chance
it was a staged romance
the whole time you were acting

My Heart – your stage
My Tears – your pen
My Trust – your page

A truth twisted is still fake
I was swept in your wake
performance improved
with each take
an expert at raising the stakes
instead of legs you're out here
causing hearts to break

My Touch – discarded
My Time – all wasted
My Soul – forever guarded

I'll never know your real character
if performance is the only factor
then you deserve an Oscar
because you are one hell of an actor

<u>Fractions</u>

I WISH you were choosing me

your body could be USING me

instead of LOOSING me

enjoying the EUPHORIA of passion

our NATURAL attraction

reduced to settling for a FRACTION

if LOVE isn't a trend

then how did we go out of FASHION?

25.   # <u>Absence</u>

My body still can't

get use to climbing

into a bed that's cold

or rolling into covers that fold

only to discover you're

not here for me to hold

your absence is my punishment

pleasurable time the has devil stole

hearts are not designed

to be placed on hold

this breakup and then makeup

game has gotten old

when jealousy infiltrated our trust

doubt completely took control

still it's impossible to separate your love

from my heart and my soul

Crossroads

Intuition told me

that something wasn't right

even though my **heart**

put up a fight

what's done in the dark

always comes to **light**

Completely blind to the **facts**

that **love** can fall

between the cracks

turn your head and it'll **slide** right through

I was oblivious to the obvious clues

now I'm stuck at the crossroads

searching for **answers**

what are you supposed to do

when the person you'd **die** for

is the same one who is **intentionally** destroying you

<u>Memory Lane</u>

Since I lost her
I haven't been the same
mind racing down memory lane
it's enough to drive a man insane
lonely hits different when you know
she's never coming back again

Love is a flame that can't be contained
same tongue that used to place the blame
was used to bite and scream my name

Trust is such an unstable thing
broken hearts can't be maintained
love is detained and feelings remain
to request and withdraw
from the same domain
knowing the whole time
peace can never be obtained

Love is a flame that can't be contained
same tongue that used to place the blame
was used to bite and scream my name

When hearts wage war in disdain
you'll always lose more than you gain
it's a shame that love gets the blame
for moves that pride should claim
thoughts of her only increase the pain
can't escape this ride down memory lane

Since I lost her
I haven't been the same
mind racing down memory lane
it's enough to drive a man insane
lonely hits different when you know
she's never coming back again

Abstract Reality

It shouldn't be a lonely bed
if it's together we sleep

hear footsteps in the dark
didn't see a need to creep

this must be a bootleg version of love
cause it feels so cheap

same house separated lives
no longer feels like home

use to be right
now it feels so wrong

it's impossible to forget
the hell we've been through

although I must admit
pieces of heaven were there too

just reflections of the past
like a mirror's shattered design

abstract reality because the truth is
you're no longer mine

Stuck On Repeat

Never **mind** the fact

that the **circle** is COMPLETE

never mind the **fact** that

another **lover** will never COMPETE

even though we're **lost** in DECEIT

my **heart** just can't RETREAT

I'm still **stuck** on REPEAT

<u>True Lies</u>

Thought I'd never say never
thought this day would never come
was a time when I used to hold you
from dusk until dawn
if passion has a light, it's no longer on
sometimes I reflect on the past
but those days are gone
the radio just stopped playing our song

Feels like time has moved against us
and now there's no more trust
I hear the urgency in your voice
but don't feel the need to rush
a whisper away from my clutch
but your body no longer calls
so I don't even touch

LOVE HAS GOTTEN BY US AND IT HAPPENED SO FAST
TRUTH IS, THE ONLY THING WE SHARE IS OUR PAST
AND IT'S JUST NOT ENOUGH TO MAKE FOREVER LAST

Let's call it a waste of potential
never a waste of time
both knew there were problems
but didn't address the signs
defeat at love or the death
of a possibility, I see
the fire has left your eyes
and you're no longer feeling me
if love is the question then
the answer is a true lie
because forever doesn't have
the option of saying goodbye

Expression 4

Featured Poem

Soul Snatching

I CAN TELL THAT YOU'VE
SECRETLY BEEN WISHING
TO HAVE A MAN THAT
CAN SCRATCH THAT ITCH
EVERYONE ELSE HAS BEEN MISSING
EXPOSING PLEASURE ZONES
THAT WERE HIDDEN
LEADING TO ERUPTIONS
IN A PARADISE OF ECSTASY GIVING
NEXT LEVEL LOVING THIS IS EXECUTIVE LIVING
SOAKED SHEETS GO FROM SATIN TO LINEN
HAVE YOU SPEAKING IN TONGUES
BEING SAVED THROUGH SINNING

Expression 4

Handcuff Heaven

Video

Poems

Staycation

Our lips keep **crashing**
tongues are clashing
with FEELINGS beyond **catching**
on an island of passion
Ms. Quiet **Storm**
we don't have to **rush**
your body is tense
and you FEEL out of touch
relax it's just us
and these sheets
VELVET **crushed**
I want to elevate your reality
then **penetrate** your fantasies
so we can bathe in a river of ecstasy
satisfy our love PROPHESY
soul kissing for an **eternity**

Your eyes are **hypnotic**
they **haunt** my dreams
that sultry voice
makes me want to **dance**
on Saturn's rings
surrendering to urges
pleasure brings SWALLOWED screams
curves **exploding** out the seams
ripped shirts and snatched jeans
embracing the wonders
of a Good Thing
we are cake and ice cream
a King's STAYCATION in
the **valley** of Queens

<u>Lip Service</u>

With these lips   With these lips   With these lips

I'll kiss your soul
make your fire rage
so your heart never gets cold
one kiss will make you lose control
create an earthquake inside your fold
cause your legs to shake and eyes to roll
switch positions so it never gets old
treasure hunting and I struck gold
scratches across my back
when you were reaching
for something to hold
an appetite for seduction
with these lips I consume
cherries, melons, and peaches whole

With these lips   With these lips   With these lips

I will infiltrate your dreams
be your love puppet
you can pull my strings
total satisfaction by any means
join the mile high club
earn your sexual wings
cascade on a river of dopamine
evoke a tornado of silent screams
these are the things
my tongue game brings
love leaves marks
like hieroglyphics on the skin
of kings and queens

With these lips   With these lips   With these lips

33. <u>Love Tornado</u>

I could walk
      through a **thunderstorm**
           with nothing on
              and use your **kisses**
                  to PROTECT from harm
                    they're all I need
                        for **peace** and calm
Lightning could **strike**
      the ground below
           caught in a love TORNADO
           I'd **never** know
              the MAN could even
                leave the **MOON**
Or if **WINTER**
      should begin in June
           no **matter** what
              the world may do
                it's IMPOSSIBLE to see
                  past **loving** you

I'll never stop loving you

          I'll never stop loving you

               I'll never stop loving you

        I will never ever stop loving you

Open The Safe

Open the safe!!
Open the safe!!
Open the safe!!

I want to know all your secrets
everything you're trying to hide
let me open your safe
and discover what's inside

Open the safe!!
Open the safe!!
Open the safe!!

It's a shame
you're holding onto so much pride
soon as I crack the code
I'm going to fill the divide
by satisfying your forbidden side

Open the safe!!
Open the safe!!
Open the safe!!

Temperature is rising
I use heat to break locks
then apply pressure nonstop
until I find your sweet spot
got the vault doors unlocked
now act like it's a stick up
give me everything you've got

Open the safe!!
Open the safe!!
Open the safe!!

Climactic

Beyond chemistry
you're guaranteed
a win with me
I'm going to
take the time
to crack the code
to your body's mystery
use its sacred pleasure key
unlock and unload the treasury
cause the gates to enter paradise
need to be opened intentionally
dive into your pool's sexual memory
mental stimulation enhances intimacy
let's push past the legacy of lust
create some sensual trust it's just us
and your body deserves justice
indulge in the hush of a euphoric rush
unleashing elevated levels of an
orgasmic crush
be careful cause next level loving
will test your sanity and this isn't vanity
certified soul snatcher, I fulfill fantasies

I'm dialed into your love sensory
you can throw away your history
nothing you've ever done intimately
compares to being skin to skin with me
you should be getting it passionately
because allowing a man to love you
casually is a pleasure tragedy
I know you came to see
if I'm everything I claim to be
ecstasy can't be reached passively
so I'll put these lips on you massively
convert your body into tsunami factory
creating ice cream dreams climactically

Handcuff Heaven

Why are you acting
like you don't know
what you came here for
always end up asking
for more of what's in store
our desires are the same
let's not play that game
tell me what you want
there's no need for shame

This attraction is
    too strong to ignore
we can take ecstasy tours
    behind closed doors
then wake up sore
    and go explore
in the wild some more

Welcome to handcuff heaven
private dance, private party
we get naughty, naughty
and roll like the mob
when it comes to moving bodies

One truth I know with certainty
is things of value are kept
under lock and key
so if your man is
leaving unlocked doors
it guarantees a robbery

<u>Sleepless</u>

On a sleepless night
I'm breakdancing in the
storm of your coffee rain
a river of fire and desire
flowing through lightning veins

melting away every single doubt
with the whisper of my name
power of the tongue
is both pleasure and pain

the thrill of the rush
enough is never enough
addicted to your paralyzing touch
need to escape before I drown
in seduction's pool of lust

You pass my fantasy tests
eyes caress and hearts confess
your kisses ignite my inner flesh
setting my soul on fire
erotic sweetness is my weakness
anticipation of elevated freakness
got me laying here sleepless

slow songs on repeat
a fistful of sheets
need to crack a window
try to free this heat
counting galaxies and heartbeats
on the sleepless night
of an orgasmic retreat

Naked Wrapture

Laying here naked
no clothes and   no covers
we don't   need them
all we need   is each other
in this moment   can we just be
unmask   your heart
and let your   truth dance free
our bodies becoming music
sound of a love symphony

Baby oil and backrubs
bliss will consume you whole
crashing lips   as kisses console
you are my   love anchor
whenever I need   someone to hold
the armor shatters   when you wrap
those comforting eyes   around my soul
the outside world   is too cold
but our windows   are open
because the temperature of hearts
has no dials and no control

Eyes blinking
thoughts   flashing
heat rising as hours are sinking
and all I want   to know is
what are   you thinking
I skydive   into your lens
our bodies   pressed together
not sure where   mine begins
but I can feel the spot where your fingertips end
stroking the keys of my piano skin
we're just taste testing an inevitable sin

<u>Indulgence</u>

Let's trade fantasies
then take trips to ecstasy
ice cream, you scream
pineapples, fudge, and whip cream
fan the steam, now lick it clean
talk to me that's what I like
can't hear you so speak to the mic
hope you're ready for a long night
I'm indulging in your moonlight
collapsing stars and galaxies all night

Don't back down now
we've come too far even though
and no one has come so far
let's make it happen
we can raise some hell
and raise the bar
Ms. Midnight star
it's time to shine
stroke so good
it'll open your nose
and the eyes of the blind
satisfaction is the plan
I want to bathe in
the raging river
of your naked skin
come up for air then
do it all over again
windows open and
sheets are wet
bodies drenched
from all the sweat
lady in the streets
ninja between the sheets
girl your secret is safe with me
just let me please you religiously

Soul Snatching

Our attraction is on me
the desire is in me
I love your energy
it magnifies our chemistry
euphoria comes through synergy
an emotional dance between
happiness and sympathy
this union is destiny
let's expand experiences and make them better
my real interest extends beyond self-pleasure
I'm determined to find your buried treasure
create an intoxicating moment that'll last forever

All men aren't built the same
some of them   have bad aim
they're shooting   for self-gain
unsatisfied passion is   hard to maintain
you're extraordinary so your
loving should never be plain
I'll try to devour you whole with no shame
your body is my business
and I ain't playing no games
I can tell that you've   secretly been wishing
to have a man that   can scratch that itch
everyone else   has been missing
exposing pleasure zones that were hidden
leading to eruptions
in a paradise of ecstasy giving
next level loving this is executive living
soaked sheets   go   from satin to linen
have you speaking in tongues being saved through sinning
neck and shoulder   action   we energy matching
our bodies   keep crashing
feelings are catching   and I'm soul snatching

Expression 5

Perfect Alignment

YOU ARE MY ANGEL

AND I WOULD TRADE HEAVEN

TO KEEP YOU GIRL

IT MAY NOT BE ETERNAL LIFE

WITH STREETS OF GOLD OR GATES OF PEARL

BUT WHEN WE'RE TOGETHER

IT'S A PERFECT WORLD

Expression 5

Bliss

Video

Poems

Anything

You can ask me any questions
I promise I won't   tell you any lies
the truth remains   the same
I need you   by my side
when it   comes to you
my heart   has no pride
so let me   make this clear
I am   digging you
and I'm willing to do **anything**
to keep you right here

Just imagine if we
only had one second together
I'd defy the   laws of physics
to treasure that   moment forever
even if it meant   stopping time
and living in   an instance
no lie you define   my existence
I'd put the earth's   rotation on decline
then pause   the Sun
so we'll   forever shine
do **anything**   in the world
so you will always be mine

Love carefully
because I'll   drown you
with a   thousand   kisses
give you stars   moons and   majestic riches
walk on   water   for love
write your   name in the cosmic   dust above
to show the   whole world   who I'm holding
but can't stop   dreaming of
anything and everything I can possibly do
I will so I can spend forever loving you
I'll never stop loving you

Bliss

Soul searching for bliss
I FOUND you and just knew
because my heart
has been waiting
for days like this
just had a taste
and I already miss your lips
it feels like
it's my soul you KISS

I'll do whatever it takes
to fulfill your heart wish
life goals and love gifts
together we can't miss
openly admit I want to ice
your RING finger and your wrist
then change your last name
I found heaven in your eyes
and I'll never be the same

Provide you COMFORTING arms
when you're feeling pain
a blanket of trust
protection from the rain
security that I'll always maintain
on this love campaign
because you calm my troubled waters
until only peace remains
love flowing through lightning veins
and I get high off your dopeness again and again
completely engulfed in your blissful reign

43.   # When Love Is Real

If I couldn't have you
I'd rather be by myself
picking up the pieces
to a broken heart
instead of dividing my love
with someone else

You can put my face on a million dollar bill
and it still wouldn't amount to the way you make me feel
nothing can or ever will compare to a love that's real

It's not about availability
because you can't choose
what's meant to be
all your wrongs
are just right for me
I've never tried to scrutinize
that's when I realized
we share a page
in the book of destiny

You can put my face on a million dollar bill
and it still wouldn't amount to the way you make me feel
nothing can or ever will compare to a love that's real

They could even name
a planet on my behalf
and it'll never equal
out in math
nothing can or ever will
compare to a love
A LOVE THAT'S REAL

Fortunate Hearts

Marriage is a **promise**
with INFINITE possibilities
the completion of a **circle** a desire for unity
it's love, **hope**, and a priceless gift
that the heart can't ignore
MARRIAGE is taking you for you
saying oh well and then
loving you some **more**

IT'S THE SOLUTION TO LOVE'S EQUATION
A REBIRTH AND A DIVINE CREATION
KEEPING EACH OTHER WARM
WHEN THE WORLD TURNS COLD
TWO HALVES BECOMING A WHOLE
THE CULMINATION OF A VOYAGE
FOR TWO SEARCHING SOULS

Marriage is the next **level**
a **commitment** to rise
the only **option** is life, it has to survive
and like a rose in the **garden** of love
it can thrive to a spiritual **perfection**
creating a place in two **fortunate** hearts
for a **divine** connection

Marriage is mental and **spiritual** unity
that **transcends** individuality
an emotional **journey** of transformation
two hearts making a commitment to patience
promising to be each other's salvation
wedding bells mark the **final** destination
a meeting of destiny that was
blessed from the start
love is the world's **greatest** fortune
because it's an investment in the **heart**

45. <u>Beyond Expectations</u>

True love is when
YOU
continue to grow
false impressions
WILL
come and go
no need to
QUESTION
because you will always know
don't even have to ask
LOVE
will always show
as the foolish assume
false hearts meet their doom
WHILE
unconditional love consumes
time slows and water flows
as flowers bloom
"I do" won't
CHANGE
in a million Junes
as long as the Sun
transforms night into day
love will be the castle
in which you stay
when a heart
ALIGNS
toward heaven's way
exceeding expectations
and saying I do
is the only price
YOU
have to pay

Vulnerable

Marriage
is being humble
and believing that love
is greater than both
never leaving the door open
to disregard your oath
taking the high road
to compromise and discipline
a circle of love
that requires less talk
and more listening
when fingertips extend
far beyond the reach of man
touching a vulnerability beneath the skin
to discover the person hiding within
where guarded walls tumble like dominos
so you advance with open palms
and extended arms leaving your heart exposed
it's trusting the person standing next to you
after they've seen the best and worst of you
and are still compelled to see it through
in fact they couldn't imagine
a world without loving you
the ultimate commitment
isn't just saying I do
it's removing your armor
and being vulnerable too

Let's be vulnerable
Let's be vulnerable
Let's be vulnerable together

47. <u>Good Thing</u>

It's funny how you can live your **entire** life
and never find that one Good Thing
someone who's presence
makes your **spirit** rise and your heart sing
few people are truly united with their soulmates
make that **absolute connection** with destiny
and control fate
most of us just **struggle** through love making do
because a lonely heart can **attach**
to just about anyone that's good people

Why do I **love** you?
If you don't know
then I'll never truly
be able to **verbally** explain
maybe it's the way you look at me
and force me to smile
or just by saying my name
sometimes I wonder
if I purposely **stumbled**
into your **galaxy** of beautiful brown eyes
I can't explain the **magnitude**
of how I'm into you
it's an **evolving** surprise

Took a crash course in **romance**
for just one **chance** to hold you close
found **bliss** before our first physical kiss
this appears to be a **spiritual** overdose
being your man is my greatest **pleasure**
and has **solved** all my unanswered questions
propelling me to the **status** of a KING

Now I know why doves cry
  and why the caged bird sings
    see my heart wasn't quite **complete**
     until I found this Good Thing
      I **believe** in my heart
       that you are my QUEEN

The only **crown** that I can offer you
  is a one of kind feeling **secured** totally
   with a sweet soulful style of loving
    it's a **distinctive** feeling that guarantees
     your heart will never again need **healing**

An **eternity** that's delivered
   in a clear glass bowl
    what you see is what you get
     but what you feel **consumes** your soul
      I'll pour it on and engulf your body
       until you're emotionally **intoxicated**
        physical is the action but spiritually
        is how I **punctuate** it

A **complex** formula that's easily equated
  a Good Thing can't be staged
  and love is the only **recipe** to create it
   it's a connection that exists **infinitely**
   and it's completely based on
    commitment and honesty

Like the **finest** wine
  it only gets **better** with time
   this works because some things
    were just meant to be
     some things just **belong** together
     like cake with ice cream
      sleep with dreams
       stars with the sky and you and I
       eternally to be
      a good thing

48. <u>Perfect Alignment</u>

You are my **angel**
and I would trade HEAVEN
to **keep** you girl

it may not be **eternal** life
with streets of **gold**
or **gates** of PEARL

but when **we're** together
it's a **perfect** world

Nothing **compares**
to your **CALMING** touch
that's just a **glimpse** of why
I **need** you so much

You can **look** through
a ball of **crystal**
and still can't **conceive**

WHAT YOUR LOVE DOES FOR ME

the stars must **align**
with the BEAT of our **hearts**

because we **share**
a **priceless** investment
in love's **work** of art

This Is Love

Love is complete when two people
dare not to compete
they compare, they share, and dance to the same beat
fall down and get back up again
then walk silently hand-in-hand
body language more verbal than any voice
it says tomorrow is our ultimate plan
where dancing eyes stand still paralyzed
in a balance between smiles and cries
because no matter what tomorrow brings
this bond is stronger than golden rings
it's when your chemistry creates
a divine connection with destiny and determines fate
saying "if you accept me as I am"
I will be your soulmate
knowing that God's will is your destiny
when you can't choose what's meant to be
"This is love"

Marriage is planting seeds on sacred ground
the location is somewhere between sight and sound
it's extending yourself and accepting a new life
an eternal connection of two families
with two words husband and wife
it's a spiritual declaration to prevail over any situation
an infinity of conscious unity enclosed in an invisible sphere
that states "this is love and envious hearts may not enter here"
a perfect contrast between bothersome and bliss
somewhere in the middle of paradise
and Momma told me there would be days like this
meeting in a moment as precise as Saturn's rings
it's impossible to act out the element of a good thing
see love never pretends it consumes then ascends
gives life and then begins again
and THIS IS LOVE

50. <u>Partners In Purpose</u>

Will you be my
Partner In Purpose?
we can make it
through this **circus**
I'm certain
let's **pull** back the curtain
and **push** past the **trappings**
of the physical
give each other **access**
to **aspects** of our lives
that are more **instrumental**
I swear we can
make happiness a **ritual**

Will you be my
Partner In Purpose
baby will you be
My Partner
In Purpose

Will you be my
Partner In Purpose
baby will you be
My Partner
In Purpose

Will you be my
Partner In Purpose
baby will you be
My Partner
In Purpose

Our only problem
should be loving **too hard**
instead of **masking** all our scars
we just play **hearts** face up
revealing all the cards
love has **layers** like **inception**
together we'll **escape** the **deception**
and discover what's **real** together
pick up the **broken** pieces
we can **heal** together
then set **goals**
we can **fulfill** together
you **speak** to my heart
and the words are
MINE FOREVER

Will you be my
Partner In Purpose
baby will you be
My Partner
In Purpose

Will you be my
Partner In Purpose
baby will you be
My Partner
In Purpose

Will you be my
Partner In Purpose
baby will you be
My Partner
In Purpose

What if we held **hands**
but our **gaze**
was even stronger
it felt so good
we just **laid** in bed
a little longer

let's allow love to be our **foundation**
and every day will be a
"my baby is the shit" **celebration**

then **together** we can build
rock that **old school** Guy
have a **glass of wine** and JUST CHILL
I **promise** to never let your kisses spill

we will always **equal** more
if we never **settle** for less
than being
Partners In Purpose

Will you be my
Partner In Purpose
baby will you be
My Partner
In Purpose

Will you be my
Partner In Purpose
baby will you be
My Partner
In Purpose

Will you be my
Partner In Purpose
baby will you be
My Partner
In Purpose

We can make it through this **circus** I'm certain

This Is Love

@Edopoetics

Lost Light

To every woman I've ever been blessed to have access to on an emotional or physical level. Thank you. Our experiences have influenced and inspired me to write this book. They have filled my emotional well and have been a resource for my creativity. Good or bad everyone from my past has helped shape me into being a better man. A more emotionally evolved man who is striving to become the best version of himself. To anyone who I've hurt in any way; I'm truly sorry and hope you can forgive me. My goal is to love my future wife honestly and completely.

So, I forgive anyone who has hurt me along the way. I also forgive myself. Life really is too short to be carrying the burden of anger and resentment. I wish you peace and happiness.

I want us all to win.

Be blessed.

ACKNOWLEDGMENTS

To my rock, Mamie "Grandma" Walker:
You are the most amazing person that I've ever met. Because of you I'm a witness to what unconditional love looks like. I believe every generation owes a debt for the sacrifices of their elders. I could live two lifetimes and wouldn't be able to repay what yours are worth.

To my Sun: Edo Walker IV
Some of these poems started out as songs that I was preparing for you since your passion for music was evident when you were a child. It's no surprise to me that you've developed into such a talented hip hop artist. I've always tried to be a living example, so you were afforded the courage to pursue your ambitions with reckless abandonment. Never give up on your dreams, always embrace your gifts, and aspire to live an authentic and impactful life. I am extremely proud of the man you have become. I love you more than life, my young Prince.

To my sister, Mamie Walker:
I love you and I miss you, baby sister. Losing you has left the impact of a meteor shower on my heart. You influenced the lives of everyone who entered your orbit. Kiss my nephew, Sage, for me. May you both Rest in Heaven, my angel.

To my circle of love:
This book would not have been possible without the support and encouragement of many friends and family who have uplifted me and some like "Footprints in the Sand" in my darkest hour even carried me along the way. I'm eternally grateful for everyone who helped me bring *Partners In Purpose* to the page.

Thank You!

Partners In Purpose

ABOUT THE AUTHOR

Edo Walker III is a North Minneapolis native who graduated from Minneapolis North High. He later helped revitalize the school's film program and taught an afterschool film class there.

He is an avid chess player and a film junkie. His passion for film led him to acting. He's appeared in numerous television shows and films. After a decade in the industry, he went onto complete a bachelor's degree in Screenwriting at Metropolitan State University. Edo also holds dual associate degrees in film for Directing and Cinematography.

Edo currently resides in Los Angeles where he works as an independent filmmaker. He considers himself an impact artist who creates content to inspire, empower, and inform.

Partners In Purpose is Edo's debut poetry collection and the first book in his Expression Poetry series.

Stay In Touch

TicTok: @Edopoetics

Instagram: @Edopoetics

FB: @Partnersinpurpose

Twitter: @Edo_Walker

Youtube: Edo Walker

Recent & Random